W9-BRS-929

# WEAPONS TECHNOLOGY

SCIENCE • TECHNOLOGY • ENGINEERING

BY MICHAEL BURGAN

CHILDREN'S PRESS®

An Imprint of Scholastic Inc.

CONTENT CONSULTANT
Matthew Lammi, Assistant Professor of Technology, Engineering & Design Education,
North Carolina State University

PHOTOS ©: cover: Jivaldi, LLC; 3: Lockheed Martin/U.S. Navy; 4 left: Heritage/Superstock, Inc.; 4 right: U.S.
Air Force/Getty Images; 5 left: Science Source; 5 right: 508 collection/Alamy Images; 6: Peter Newark Military
Pictures/Bridgeman Images; 8: The Granger Collection; 9: DEA/A. DAGLI ORTI/Getty Images; 10: Erich Lessing/
Art Resource, NY; 11: Taylor Davidson/EyeEm/Getty Images; 12 left: ullstein bild/Getty Images; 12 right:
The Granger Collection; 13 top: Science Museum/SSPL/The Image Works; 13 bottom: FPG/Getty Images;
14: Heritage/Superstock, Inc.; 15: General Photographic Agency/Getty Images; 16 top: Everett Collection
Historical/Alamy Images; 16 bottom: Keystone/Getty Images; 17 top: U.S. Air Force; 17 bottom: Keystone/
Getty Images; 18: Schultz Reinhard/Prisma/Superstock, Inc.; 19: Everett Collection Historical/Alamy Images;
20: U.S. Air Force/Getty Images; 22: andrew chittock/Alamy Images; 23: Mass Communication Specialist
3rd Class Jonathan Sunderman/U.S. Navy; 24: Erik Simonsen/Getty Images; 25: Mass Communications
Specialist 2nd Class Jason R. Zalasky/U.S. Navy; 26 left: John Frost Newspapers/Alamy Images; 26 right: John
Williams/U.S. Navy; 27 top: Flirt/Alamy Images; 27 bottom: John F. Williams/U.S. Navy; 28: MILpictures
by Tom Weber/Getty Images; 29: AFP/Getty Images; 30 left: Everett Collection/Superstock, Inc.; 30 right-31
left: Everett Collection/Superstock, Inc.; 31 right: Everett Collection Historical/Alamy Images; 32: Mariana
Bazo/Reuters; 33: Bloomberg/Getty Images; 34: Science Source; 36: Photo Researchers/Getty Images; 37:
Production Perig/Shutterstock, Inc.; 40: JERILEE BENNETT/KRRT/Newscom; 41: Mass Communication Specialist
1st Class Eric Garst/U.S. Navy; 42 top: Bloomberg/Getty Images; 42 bottom-43 left: Mario Anzuoni/Reuters;
43 right: AMELIE-BENOIST / BSIP/Superstock, Inc.; 44: Lachlan Bucknall/Alamy Images; 45: Patti McConville/
Alamy Images; 46: Lockheed Martin/U.S. Navy; 48: U.S. Air Force photo/Staff Sgt. Aaron D. Allmon II/DVIDS;
49: Stocktrek Images/Superstock, Inc.; 50 top: Arnold Engineering Development Complex/U.S. Air Force; 50
bottom: MC Images/Alamy Images; 51 top: Mass Communication Specialist 3rd Class Timothy M. Ahearn/U.S.
Navy; 51 bottom: 508 collection/Alamy Images; 52: Mass Communication Specialist Seaman Zhiwei Tan/U.S.
Navy; 53: Johann Brandstatter/Alamy Images; 54 left: Everett Collection Historical/Alamy Images; 54 right-55
left: THOMAS COEX/Getty Images; 55 right: MILITARY, ARMY, NAVY/Alamy Images; 56: Sergio Azenha/Alamy
Images; 57: The Washington Post/Getty Images; 58: Z2A1/Alamy Images; 59 top: Department of Defense/
Marvin Lynchard/Flickr; 59 bottom: Stocktrek Images/Media Bakery.

LIBRARY OF CONGRESS CATALOGING-IN-PUBLICATION DATA
Names: Burgan, Michael, author.
Title: Weapons technology : science, technology, and engineering / by Michael Burgan.
Other titles: Calling all innovators.
Description: New York,. NY : Children's Press, an imprint of Scholastic Inc.,
   [2016] | Series: Calling all innovators: a career for you? | Includes
   bibliographical references and index.
Identifiers: LCCN 2015045201| ISBN 9780531218914 (library binding) | ISBN
   9780531219911 (pbk.)
Subjects: LCSH: Weapons—Juvenile literature. | Weapons industry—Vocational
   guidance—Juvenile literature. | Military art and science—Juvenile literature.
Classification: LCC UF500 .B874 2016 | DDC 623.4—dc23
LC record available at http://lccn.loc.gov/2015045201

All rights reserved. Published in 2017 by Children's Press, an imprint of Scholastic Inc.
Printed in the United States of America 113

1 2 3 4 5 6 7 8 9 10 R 26 25 24 23 22 21 20 19 18 17

Science, technology, engineering, the arts, and math are the fields that drive innovation. Whether they are finding ways to make our lives easier or developing the latest entertainment, the people who work in these fields are changing the world for the better. Do you have what it takes to join the ranks of today's greatest innovators? Read on to discover if a career in the exciting world of weapons technology is for you.

# TABLE *of* CONTENTS

Airplanes were first used in combat during World War I.

Many of the latest weapons rely on robotics technology.

*Uncrewed aircraft called drones are often used in today's military conflicts.*

*Engineers and scientists perform many tests on new weapons before they are used on the battlefield.*

Tanks were one of the greatest military innovations of the 20th century.

TREADS ALLOW TANK TO MOVE EASILY OVER TRENCHES AND HILLS

DRIVERS PROTECTED BY TANK'S ARMOR

1

# THE TOOLS OF WAR

German soldiers looked up from the trenches in amazement as a new weapon moved toward them. The oddly shaped metal vehicle could roll over almost any surface. Inside, British soldiers drove the vehicle and operated its machine gun. On September 15, 1916, the Germans saw a tank enter battle for the first time.

World War I had been going on for just over two years. While the war spanned many countries, some of the heaviest fighting took place in France, where French and British forces joined together against the Germans. The British wanted an armored vehicle that could cross trenches and other enemy defenses. The tank filled this role perfectly. Its wide treads could roll over obstacles that would stop a wheeled vehicle in its tracks. The tank's heavy armor protected the soldiers inside. One British soldier said the Germans "bolted like rabbits" when they saw the new weapon.

## BIG STEPS FORWARD

| 1836 | 1862 | 1884 | 1916 |
|------|------|------|------|
| Samuel Colt introduces the revolver handgun. | Warships are covered with iron for protection. | The first fully automatic machine gun is invented. | Tanks are used in battle for the first time. |

# MEETING NEW CHALLENGES

Throughout history, the outbreak of war—or the desire to prevent one—has led scientists, engineers, and other innovators to seek new and better weapons of all kinds. The British engineers who designed the first tank were responding to changes in warfare. Soldiers had fought from trenches before. However, World War I saw huge numbers of soldiers fighting from those trenches for months at a time. British military leaders hoped tanks would give them an advantage against the Germans. But the first tanks had problems that kept them from being perfect weapons. For one thing, they were slow. Engineers tried building lighter tanks that moved faster, but the lighter armor was too thin to protect the soldiers inside. In later years, engineers improved tank designs, and they became major weapons in several wars.

*Trenches were dug to make it easier for soldiers to stay out of the way of gunfire.*

*Many ancient weapons were made by forming blades out of stone.*

# THE FIRST WEAPONS

Weapons are not a recent invention. Ancient humans used wooden spears to hunt several hundred thousand years ago. They also made clubs from wood and rocks, and later sharpened stones to use as spearheads and arrowheads. The next advancement came when people learned to shape metal into knives and swords. Metal weapons were sharper and lighter than ones made from stone.

People also used weapons to battle each other. Evidence of the first war between groups of people dates back about 13,000 years. War became more common as humans settled down, began farming, and built cities. One ruler might want another ruler's land or resources. Early armies relied on swords, spears, axes, and arrows.

The development of gunpowder marked a move toward more modern war. This explosive substance is a mixture of several chemicals. The earliest recorded recipe for gunpowder was created in China during the 11th century. This discovery eventually led to many new kinds of weapons.

FUSE

EXPLOSION FROM
GUNPOWDER

PROJECTILE

*The early gun technology that developed in China eventually spread to Europe and other parts of the world.*

## MOVING TOWARD MODERN WARFARE

Chinese fighters first used gunpowder by packing it into paper
packets and attaching a fuse. A soldier lit the fuse and then fired the
packet at the enemy using an arrow. Once the fuse burned down to
the gunpowder, the packet exploded. Later, the Chinese learned that
a tube filled with burning gunpowder could be fired without a bow.
The gunpowder created gases when it burned, and the force of those
gases shooting out of the back of the tube could launch the tube
through the air. This discovery led to the first rockets. The Chinese
also determined that gunpowder's explosive force could launch
objects out of metal or clay tubes. They used this technique to fire
stone and metal **projectiles** at enemy forces.

The idea of using gunpowder to shoot projectiles led to the first
cannons and guns. As technology improved, these weapons became
a major part of warfare. Gun makers designed **artillery** that could
fire solid metal balls or exploding **shells**. These huge cannons were
moved onto the battlefield by horses or groups of men. Navies also
began equipping their ships with cannons.

# GREATER GUNS

Another improvement was the development of breech-loading guns and artillery. Instead of putting a bullet or shell down the front of the barrel, soldiers armed the weapon from an opening at the back of the barrel. This allowed for faster reloading. Another improvement was rifling, or cutting a spiral groove inside a gun or cannon barrel. That made a projectile more accurate after it was fired. Rifling became common after 1850.

Along with making guns more accurate, military engineers designed guns that could fire many bullets rapidly. The first of these machine guns required a soldier to turn a crank to add more bullets. During the 1880s, Hiram Maxim perfected the first automatic machine gun. Some of the power of the explosion that propelled a bullet also fed the next bullet to be fired. This allowed soldiers to fire round after round by simply holding down a gun's trigger.

Hiram Maxim poses with one of his machine guns.

BULLETS ATTACHED TO A LONG BELT

EMPTY BULLET CASINGS

*John Holland peers out from the entrance of one of his submarines.*

## WARFARE UNDER THE SEA

In addition to the introduction of the tank, World War I also saw the first widespread use of a new kind of warship: the submarine. For several hundred years, inventors had been working to create a vessel that traveled underwater. Simple early submarines were put to use in the American Civil War. John Holland created the first successful modern submarine in 1898 in the United States. His design influenced many of the subs used during World War I.

## SUBMARINE SCIENCE

Holland was a schoolteacher, not a trained engineer or scientist. However, he had an interest in both science and engineering. Holland knew that the key to building an underwater vessel was overcoming buoyancy. This force occurs in a liquid when an object less dense than the liquid is placed on its surface. Buoyancy makes the object float. A submarine uses extra weight, called ballast, to overcome buoyancy and sink below the water's surface. Releasing the ballast allows the sub to come back to the surface. Holland's sub was equipped with tanks that held water, which served as the ballast. The tanks were emptied or filled to adjust the sub's depth.

*As this cutaway illustration shows, the interiors of submarines can be very cramped.*

*Crew members stand atop a partially submerged submarine in 1901.*

## FAST AND DANGEROUS

Holland also used dual **propulsion**—his subs had one power system for traveling on the surface and another for moving underwater. The surface power came from a gas engine, while a battery-powered engine propelled the sub underwater. To make the sub useful in combat, Holland equipped it with torpedoes. These self-propelled rockets had already been used on traditional warships. But by traveling underwater, a sub could approach an enemy ship unseen before firing its torpedoes.

## SEARCHING FOR SUBS

Submarines proved to be effective weapons during World War I. To help surface ships defend themselves, scientists developed a way to use sound waves to locate subs underwater. The waves hit an object and then returned to the ship that generated them. The system for finding subs and other underwater objects is called sound navigation and ranging—or "sonar" for short. ☀

*An airplane is launched from a British submarine during World War I.*

FLOATS ALLOW AIRPLANES TO LAND ON WATER

# 20TH-CENTURY ADVANCEMENTS

Tanks and submarines weren't the only new weapons to be introduced during World War I. It was also during this time that airplanes were first used for combat. Brothers Orville and Wilbur Wright had completed the first-ever airplane flight in 1903, just 11 years before the war started. Almost immediately, military leaders saw that planes could have many uses in battle. Pilots could use them to observe enemy activities or drop bombs from the sky. As bomber planes became common during the war, air forces developed fighter planes to defend against attacks from above. These planes were equipped with machine guns to shoot bombers down. Armies also developed special artillery designed to fire into the air.

*Airplane battles are also known as "dogfights."*

## ROBERT GODDARD

When the United States entered World War I in 1917, physicist Robert Goddard (1882–1945) began working to improve the military's rocket technology. Goddard was studying new kinds of fuels for rockets besides gunpowder. In 1926, he launched the first rocket to be fueled by liquid chemicals. It reached an **altitude** of just 41 feet (12 meters). Goddard continued to improve liquid fuel rockets, building some that could reach an altitude of almost 2 miles (3 kilometers) and travel at speeds of more than 700 miles (1,127 km) per hour. His work led to more powerful military rockets and to the rockets used to put astronauts into space. He has been called the father of modern rocketry.

*German soldiers wear gas masks to protect themselves from chemical weapons as they fire an antiaircraft gun.*

## IMPROVING OLDER WEAPONS

World War I and the following years also saw engineers continuing to improve the technology behind older weapons. Machine guns became lighter so they could easily be carried and operated by a single soldier. Mortars, a form of artillery that had been used for several hundred years, became smaller. A soldier could easily set up and fire a mortar, which usually launched an exploding shell.

The first large-scale use of chemical weapons occurred during World War I, when the German military used them in 1915. Before long, many other countries were releasing deadly chemicals over battlefields. As often happens in military science, armies created ways to protect themselves from these new offensive weapons. Soon soldiers were equipped with masks containing special substances to counter the effects of the enemy's chemical weapons.

# FIRST THINGS FIRST

## DETECTION AND DEFLECTION

During World War II (1939–1945), militaries relied heavily on radar technology to track the movement of enemy airplanes. Developed by British researchers, radar is very similar to sonar. The main difference is that it uses radio waves instead of sound waves. As militaries began finding more and more new uses for radar, it became one of the most important technologies introduced during the war.

*U.S. sailors examine a radar display during World War II.*

## DEFEATING RADAR

Once a new military invention appears on the battlefield, scientists and engineers look for a way to defeat it or make it less effective. Naturally, this happened as soon as radar began making air attacks more difficult. Militaries began working to create **stealth** technology to help prevent airplanes and other objects from appearing on enemy radar systems. For example, special paints were designed that would absorb radio waves rather than bounce them back to their source.

*The British military used radar devices like this one to detect enemy planes.*

The B-2 Spirit is a stealth plane that is able to drop bombs from above without being detected.

After the war, the United States took the lead in stealth technology. One of its early successes was the SR-71 Blackbird spy plane. Certain pieces of the plane's exterior were angled so they would not bounce radio signals back to their source.

## STAYING OUT OF SIGHT

By the 1980s, the United States had built stealth fighters and bomber planes. They were designed to misdirect or absorb radar. To be even stealthier, they were also built to give off less heat. This helped the planes avoid heat-seeking missiles. Modern stealth planes are also designed to fly at night, when dark skies provide natural cover. Today, militaries around the world continue to improve stealth technology and have adapted it for use on helicopters and warships. ☀

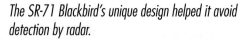

The SR-71 Blackbird's unique design helped it avoid detection by radar.

*The nuclear bomb dropped on Hiroshima, Japan, left the city almost completely destroyed.*

## THE WEAPONS OF WORLD WAR II

As with World War I, World War II resulted in the creation of many new and improved weapons. Germany flew the first plane powered by a jet engine, which could go faster than planes with conventional engines. Germany also used a long-range, liquid-fueled rocket called the V2 to attack British targets. The V2 was the first guided missile. A simple computer on board was programmed to take the rocket to its target. **Gyroscopes** detected any straying from the path and made adjustments to the rocket's course.

The most powerful invention of the war was the atomic bomb. Just before the war, scientists had learned that splitting the **atoms** of certain materials released tremendous amounts of energy. With that knowledge, U.S. researchers developed the first atomic bomb. The ones dropped on the Japanese cities of Hiroshima and Nagasaki near the end of World War II destroyed huge parts of the cities and killed tens of thousands of people. Those bombs and other weapons like it are called **nuclear** weapons.

# AFTER WORLD WAR II

The helicopter, which was first widely used during the Korean War (1950–1953), improved battlefield medicine. These aircraft could quickly retrieve wounded soldiers and bring them to a hospital. As helicopters became faster and larger, they also carried machine guns and rockets to attack enemy troops.

After World War II, the United States competed in an arms race with its main rival, the Soviet Union. Each side sought to improve on the weapons developed during the war. That meant building larger and more accurate rockets, faster jet planes, and more powerful atomic weapons. The drive to create move effective weapons continues today in countries around the world.

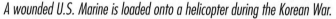

*A wounded U.S. Marine is loaded onto a helicopter during the Korean War.*

Militaries are relying more and more on robots to complete important jobs, many of which would be dangerous for humans.

# CHAPTER TWO

# THE SEARCH FOR BETTER WEAPONS

Tomorrow's wars could look much different from the ones we are used to seeing. Thanks to robots called fully **autonomous** weapons (FAWs), the need for human soldiers on the battlefield may one day be greatly reduced. FAWs will contain computers that can be programmed to carry out different kinds of missions. These robots will also be capable of adjusting plans and making spur-of-the-moment decisions as the situation changes during a mission.

The idea of military robots that can make their own decisions may sound like science fiction. But several countries are already developing weapons that are partially autonomous. Others are dedicating huge resources to creating FAWs. One day, wars could be fought entirely by FAWs instead of human soldiers.

## RECENT BREAKTHROUGHS

| 2001 | 2009 | 2011 | 2014 | 2015 |
|---|---|---|---|---|
| A drone fires a missile for the first time. | The U.S. Navy begins building a stealth warship. | A Blackhawk stealth helicopter is used in combat for the first time. | The U.S. Navy tests a laser weapon at sea. | The U.S. Army tests a weapon system that shoots down enemy drones. |

# THE ROAD TO ROBOTS

It will be many years before FAWs become a common part of military operations. Creating a FAW will require improvements in artificial intelligence—the ability of computers to "think" on their own. However, less advanced robots are already being used on the battlefield today.

Small robots with tanklike treads can be remotely controlled to look for bombs hidden under roads. They can also be equipped with cameras and sensors to observe enemy movement. The U.S. Army is working on new military robots for another use: carrying wounded soldiers off the battlefield. Flying robots could be used to carry medical equipment to troops operating behind enemy lines.

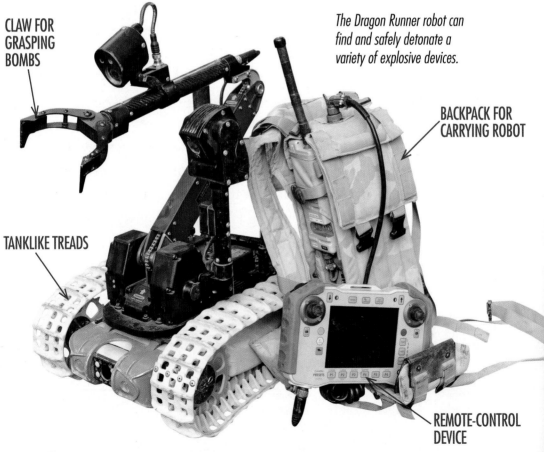

CLAW FOR GRASPING BOMBS

TANKLIKE TREADS

*The Dragon Runner robot can find and safely detonate a variety of explosive devices.*

BACKPACK FOR CARRYING ROBOT

REMOTE-CONTROL DEVICE

*Many naval ships are equipped with guided cruise missiles.*

## CRUISING AT HIGH SPEED

Military technology, like science and technology in general, often builds on existing ideas and inventions. One recent example of this is the U.S. Air Force's efforts to make faster cruise missiles. Cruise missiles have been used for several decades. These missiles fly close to the ground to avoid enemy radar. They are powered by small **turbine** engines similar to the ones used in airplanes. The engines can produce speeds of about 500 miles (805 km) per hour.

In 2015, several companies were building more powerful turbine engines for U.S. cruise missiles. These engines will propel the missiles at more than 2,000 miles (3,219 km) per hour. The trick for engineers is to make sure a missile can still be carefully guided without crashing at such high speeds. Military experts suggest that these improved cruise missiles will also have stealth features.

An artist's rendition shows what HELLADS might look like in action.

# LEADING THE WAY WITH LASERS

Military scientists and engineers are always looking for new ways to use existing technologies on the battlefield. One current example of this is the attempt to build powerful weapons using laser technology. Inside a laser beam, atoms of certain materials receive doses of electrical energy. This causes them to release energy in the form of light. That light energy is concentrated into a beam that can be used for many purposes. For example, lasers play important roles in certain kinds of surgery. They are also used to cut hard substances such as metals.

Many militaries are working to create laser beams powerful enough to destroy enemy targets. For example, the U.S. Air Force is developing a project called the High Energy Liquid Laser Area Defense System (HELLADS). The HELLADS is a powerful, yet small and light, laser that can be attached to an airplane. A pilot could use the HELLADS to shoot down enemy missiles. The laser could also be used to attack targets on the ground.

# LIGHT AND SOUND

In 2014, the U.S. Navy revealed its own laser device, the Laser Weapon System (LaWS). Batteries power the laser, which in tests has already shot down drones and blasted a huge hole in a ship. As long as the laser has enough battery power, the laser has an unlimited source of ammunition to fire at enemy targets.

Sound waves are another common form of energy that can be used as a weapon. Sound that is very loud or high-pitched can cause pain in humans. A weapon called a Long Range Acoustic Device (LRAD) emits high levels of these sounds. It can direct the waves of energy at a specific target, instead of sending the waves off in all directions. At sea, LRADs have been used to stop pirates from boarding ships.

*U.S. Navy sailors use an LRAD device to combat a group of pirates in 2009.*

SOUND WAVES ARE EMITTED BY LRAD

## BUILDING A SUPERGUN

During the two world wars of the 20th century, Germany built the largest guns the world had ever seen. Like artillery, they fired shells packed with gunpowder. These "superguns" had extremely long barrels—more than 100 feet (30 m) long—and they could hit targets from many miles away.

*A projectile is fired from an electromagnetic railgun.*

## A NEW APPROACH

In recent years, the U.S. Navy has been working on its own supergun. Unlike the German ones, the navy's gun will be small enough to be mounted on a ship. And unlike other traditional artillery, the new gun uses electricity instead of an explosion to fire its projectiles.

As its name suggests, the electromagnetic railgun relies on both electricity and magnetism. The electricity creates magnetic fields that are used to slide a metal device called an armature

*The German military used its superguns to attack London, England, during World War II.*

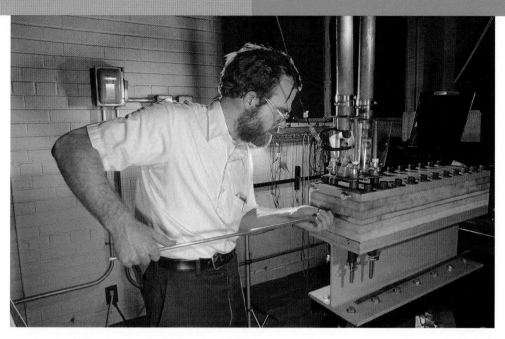

*An engineer conducts tests on an electromagnetic railgun.*

back and forth between two rails. The energy created by the moving armature can then launch a projectile at speeds of up to 4,500 miles (7,242 km) per hour over a distance of 100 miles (161 km). It is the extreme speed of the projectile that creates damage when it hits its target, rather than the explosion created by standard artillery shells. The railgun's projectiles will also carry guidance systems that help them hit their targets. Current railguns face technological limitations. However, when the Navy perfects the gun, it hopes to be able to fire 10 projectiles per minute at targets both on land and at sea.

## SAFETY AT SEA

The Navy believes that using a nonexplosive projectile will help protect its sailors because the projectiles can't accidentally explode onboard. And because the projectiles don't explode, there is no risk that they might harm people who later come across them at the site of a battle. ✷

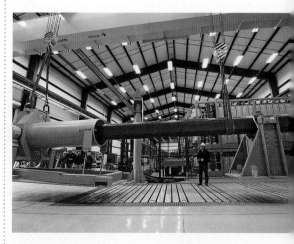

*Electromagnetic railguns are very heavy and must be lifted using cranes.*

# COURSE CORRECTION

Cruise missiles and other guided weapons have been in use for many years. However, these are large weapons meant for targets such as vehicles and buildings. But what if similar technology could be applied to the weapons carried by soldiers on the ground? The new "smart" bullet the U.S. government announced in 2015 does exactly that. Once fired, this bullet can change course in midair to hit its target. Sensors and a guidance system in the bullet tell it where it should go. The bullet can also detect weather conditions that might make it drift off target and then use this information to adjust its path. This advanced ammunition was designed for snipers, who often aim at targets as far as 2,000 feet (610 m) away. The smart bullet will let them accurately shoot from more than three times that distance.

*New technology could make it easier for snipers to hit targets from great distances.*

SPOTTER USES BINOCULARS TO HELP SNIPER LOCATE TARGETS

SILENCER HELPS MUFFLE THE SOUND OF GUNFIRE

TRIPOD HELPS KEEP GUN STABLE

ADS systems are mounted on armored trucks so they can be brought wherever they are needed.

# A NEW KIND OF AMMUNITION

In 2015, the Russian military announced it was developing a new kind of gun that doesn't use bullets or shells at all. Instead, it fires a burst of microwave energy. The microwaves can shut down the electronics used to guide enemy drones and missiles. The gun's energy can disable its targets from about 6 miles (10 km) away.

The United States has tested a similar energy-based weapon. The Active Denial System (ADS) uses energy similar to microwaves. However, this energy doesn't go as deep into the objects it enters. The waves from the ADS heat up the surface of whatever they touch. The system is designed to hold back violent civilians without killing them. As their bodies heat up from the ray, the human targets quickly move out of the weapon's range. The ADS's energy can cover a distance of about 3,000 feet (914 m).

# FROM THIS TO THAT

*Nuclear explosions produce "mushroom clouds," which are named for their shape.*

## FROM REAL EXPLOSIONS TO COMPUTER SIMULATIONS

Testing is a major part of designing and building a new weapon. For many years, this meant that researchers had to detonate dangerous bombs in order to observe the results. During World War II, scientists working for the U.S. government built the world's first atomic bomb. They knew in theory that it would work. However, they had to detonate a test bomb to make sure they hadn't made any mistakes. To do this, they found a remote location in New Mexico where the explosion would not harm anyone. The test took place on July 16, 1945, and went exactly as planned.

## A BIGGER BOMB

After World War II, the United States tested nuclear bombs that join together atoms of hydrogen. That process releases even larger amounts of energy than an atomic bomb. Testing hydrogen bombs, however, released large amounts of radiation—a form of energy that can be harmful or even deadly in large doses—into the

environment. In 1963, the United States, Great Britain, and the Soviet Union agreed to stop testing these bombs in the air, underwater, or in space. They could still test them underground, if the radiation did not drift outside of the country that was performing the tests.

*President John F. Kennedy signs the nuclear-test ban treaty in 1963.*

*The Z Machine can produce temperatures hotter than the insides of stars.*

# TESTING IN THE LAB

In 1992, the United States stopped all test explosions of nuclear weapons. Instead, nuclear weapons are now tested using computer **simulations** and laboratory experiments. Scientists run these tests at several government labs. They make sure that new weapons will work correctly. They also ensure that older bombs are still reliable and safe to handle.

Understanding the physics of how the weapons work is key for the scientists carrying out the simulations. Helping them are tools such as the Z Machine at Sandia National Laboratories in Albuquerque, New Mexico. This device produces large amounts of radiation and helps scientists understand how different materials would be affected by a nuclear blast. ✳

VIDEO SCREEN
SHOWS WHAT
CROWS IS
POINTING AT

JOYSTICK USED TO
CONTROL CROWS

*A U.S. soldier operates a CROWS system in Afghanistan.*

## THE VIRTUAL BATTLEFIELD

Many current weapons systems, along with those under
development, rely on computers to work. Advanced computer
**software** is at the heart of the Common Remotely Operated
Weapon Station (CROWS). The system is mounted on top of
small armored vehicles. Soldiers inside a CROWS-equipped vehicle
watch a video screen and control the system with a joystick. This
allows them to stay safely in the vehicle as they fire its weapons. The
CROWS can carry a number of different weapons, such as machine
guns or grenade launchers.

The CROWS has been called a video game with real guns.
Programs similar to video games are also part of the technology the
U.S. military uses to train soldiers. Training software is often used
to teach soldiers how to pilot planes and other vehicles. Virtual
reality software is used to help soldiers prepare for a wide variety of
combat situations.

# COMBAT COMPUTERS

Computers are a vital part of modern defense systems. Today, militaries around the world work to prevent cyberattacks, or attacks through computer networks. These attacks are sometimes carried out by nations. Other times they come from private groups. Cyberattacks are usually used to steal information. Along with preventing these attacks, military computer experts try to collect electronic information from their enemies. The United States, for example, looks for information that terrorists share about their future plans.

With 3D printers, computers are also being used to design and manufacture important tools on the battlefield. These printers make it easier for soldiers to make objects for field use right on the spot, rather than waiting for them to be shipped from their home countries. In 2015, the British Navy tested a drone made by a 3D printer. The printer produced four separate parts that could be assembled without any tools. The drone had a 4-foot (1.2 m) wingspan and could fly at 60 miles (97 km) per hour.

*A 3D-printed drone is displayed at the 2015 Dubai Air Show in the United Arab Emirates.*

The RQ-4 Global Hawk is an uncrewed aircraft used by the U.S. Air Force for reconnaissance.

# WEAPON MAKERS AT WORK

An enemy drone circles above a battlefield. To the soldiers below, the drone is a threat, whether it is simply carrying out **reconnaissance** or preparing to attack. They need a way to shoot it down before it gets too close.

In 2015, soldiers tested a weapons system capable of hitting a drone from more than 1 mile (1.6 km) away. A common artillery cannon fires a guided missile. Computers on the ground track the drone and send information to the missile using radio signals. The missile has thrusters that help it change course and reach its target. A signal from the ground detonates the missile as it approaches the drone. Because most of the electronics are on the ground, the missile is lightweight and inexpensive to build. This system was first designed to protect against incoming rockets or artillery shells. The 2015 tests showed its power to protect soldiers from drones, too.

## ATOMIC ADVANCEMENTS

| 1938–39 | 1945 | 1952 | 1987 |
| --- | --- | --- | --- |
| European scientists split atoms and release energy in the process, leading to nuclear weapons. | The United States drops two atomic bombs on Japan. | The United States tests the more powerful hydrogen bomb. | The United States and the Soviet Union agree to begin disposing of some of their nuclear weapons. |

## JOINING THE TEAM

Building modern weapons like the anti-drone system is a team effort. It draws on the work of both government agencies and private companies. For the anti-drone project, scientists and engineers had to design and build a computer system, an explosive warhead, and the missile itself. In such complex projects, these different parts are often created at separate factories and labs across the country.

Scientists who work on military weapons systems must get something called security clearance, even if they are not working directly for the government. That means they are allowed to see the military secrets they need to perform their jobs. The U.S. government has a wide range of clearance levels. These levels determine the kinds of information a worker is allowed to access. The Department of Defense, which oversees the U.S. military, has three levels: confidential, secret, and top secret.

*The Pentagon in Arlington, Virginia, is the headquarters of the U.S. Department of Defense.*

*Working in the field of national security requires an extensive interview and background-check process.*

## BACKGROUND CHECKS

The government wants to make sure people working on a weapons project are not going to share secrets with possible enemies, whether on purpose or by accident. To help keep sensitive information under wraps, background checks are conducted on all prospective employees before they are allowed to work on weapons projects.

The check for a security clearance measures a person's loyalty to the United States and ensures that they do not have ties to another nation. The check also looks into such things as the person's past criminal activity, if any, and whether they use or have used illegal drugs. A history of mental health problems could prevent someone from getting a clearance. So could being in debt. A person with debts might be tempted to take money from an enemy in exchange for military secrets.

# AN INTERVIEW WITH AEROSPACE ENGINEER TERRY JORDAN-CUTLER

*Terry Jordan-Cutler is an engineer in the Aerospace Systems Analysis Department at Sandia National Laboratories.*

**When did you start thinking about your area of engineering as a career?** I liked math and I liked the physical sciences. About the time I was a senior in high school, I decided that I'd like to learn how airplanes flew, so it seemed natural to start in aerospace engineering. So, I enrolled in aerospace engineering at Texas A&M University.

**What kind of classes did you take to prepare for your career?** I took all of the math courses I could at my high school. I also took two years of chemistry and one year of physics in high school. In college, all engineers have four semesters of math required. Also required are chemistry and physics. Most engineers take statics and dynamics, which teach the fundamentals of engineering mechanics for static (nonmoving) and dynamic (motion-based) systems.

**What other projects and jobs helped you prepare you for what you do now?** I did several science fair projects in elementary school. I was in the math club during high school. During college, I was a student member of the American Institute of Aeronautics and Astronautics (AIAA). This group helped prepare students to understand what career they might choose by bringing in engineers from industry or government to talk about their work.

I was also a cooperative education, or co-op, student during my undergrad years. The co-op program matched students to companies. I worked at NASA Johnson Space Center in Clear Lake City, Texas. I worked on some flight-simulation computer programs that were used to predict the path of the space shuttle for flight tests. It was a good introduction to some of the work of a flight dynamicist.

**What is the best path to a career in your field?** The best way to become an aerospace engineer is to take courses in aerospace engineering and get your degree in it. That said, I have worked with some folks in aerospace engineering who have degrees in mechanical engineering, physics, math, and electrical engineering.

Usually, those people have taken additional courses outside their degree program in aerospace engineering.

**Do you have a particular project that you're especially proud of, or that really took your work to another level?** MaST, or the Maneuvering Systems Technology program: I worked on the aerodynamics and flight dynamics of this project. This was a unique flight test where Sandia National Laboratories flew three re-entry vehicles. I worked on this project for many years. I enjoyed being able to learn more about the entire system, making presentations to the entire community, and gaining relationships that became useful later in my career. I enjoyed knowing enough about the system to be considered the go-to person in the room to answer questions about aerodynamics and flight dynamics for the system.

**It takes an entire team to do research or design a weapons system. Does working as a team come naturally for you?** I think that many engineers enjoy working by themselves; they like to have quiet time to figure out a problem, to dig deep into the details. However, most systems are complex and require an entire team of engineers to design the system and solve the problems that arise. I am like most engineers in that I enjoy having my quiet time to work on a problem, time to check that it is right, and time to write a report or presentation to be able to explain the work to others.

**What would your dream job be, if you were given unlimited resources?** My dream job would be to be able to pick the best, brightest, and most amiable team to work with to create flight vehicles.

**What advice would you give a young person who wants to pursue a career in your field?** Take as much math as you possibly can. You should also enjoy some of the sciences. Pursue engineering because you want to find out how things work, you are curious about the operation of things around you. No matter how book smart you are, engineering is hard, so realize that there are many engineers who went before you who didn't give up just because it was hard. ✳

Night-vision goggles help militaries carry out secret operations in the dark.

# ELECTRICAL ENGINEERING

The scientists, engineers, and other workers who design weapons specialize in a number of different fields. Each of them offers a different range of knowledge that can be applied to a project.

Modern military weapons rely heavily on sensors and other electronics to detect enemy weapons and control onboard computers, among other tasks. A background in electrical engineering gives scientists the skills they need for this kind of work. Electrical engineers might study such things as photonics—the behavior of particles of light. Photonics shapes the development of such devices as night vision goggles, lasers, guidance systems for missiles, and communication systems. Electrical engineers are also working to build sensors that detect the presence of harmful biological weapons.

# PHYSICS

Physicists study a broad range of subjects that can apply to weapons technology. One of these is aeronautics, the science of how objects fly. A plane, drone, or helicopter interacts with four forces while in flight: drag, lift, thrust, and gravity. Military scientists and engineers working with aircraft must consider those forces when figuring how fast a craft might fly and how powerful an engine needs to be to reach that goal.

Another area of physics crucial to the military is ballistics, the study of how a projectile behaves as it travels. Ballistics applies to large rockets and common bullets. Especially important is predicting the **trajectory** of a projectile. This information is needed to accurately aim a weapon.

SMOKE TRAIL SHOWS
TRAJECTORY OF MISSILE

*A guided missile is launched from a U.S. aircraft carrier.*

# THE ARTISTIC SIDE

## VIRTUAL WEAPONS

While scientists and engineers design military technology for potential battles, weapons can provide inspiration to artists. For example, talented people known as weapons artists create detailed 3D models of weapons for use in video games. Anytime you drive a tank or pilot a fighter plane in a game, you are seeing the work of these amazing artists.

## FROM THE PAGE TO THE SCREEN

To create 3D models, the artists might begin by sketching out their ideas on paper. To convert these ideas into 3D models, they use

*In the latest virtual reality games, you can get a closer look at virtual weapons than ever before.*

polygons as building blocks. A polygon is a two-dimensional shape made out of straight lines. The artists connect these 2D shapes to create a 3D image on the computer screen. A detailed model might contain thousands or even millions of polygons.

## BLENDING REALITY AND FANTASY

Because video games do not have to be realistic, artists don't have to consider scientific principles the way real weapons designers do. In some cases, artists might use a real weapon as the source for an idea. Then they have the freedom to modify its look to fit the feel of the game without

*3D modelers rely on special software to create their designs.*

worrying about whether the design would work in real life.

## LEARNING TO MAKE WEAPONS

Weapons artists usually have a background in art and design. They also must master the various software used to design 3D models. Some colleges offer degrees in digital design. The best weapons artists study the history of weapons and often have an interest in the military. ✳

*Creative game designers can create futuristic weapons unlike anything that currently exists in the real world.*

# BIOCHEMISTRY AND MATERIAL SCIENCE

Biochemistry is the study of how chemical reactions affect living creatures. Some militaries and terrorist groups use harmful **bacteria** and viruses as weapons. The United States does not use such biological weapons. However, biochemists working for the military still must study them in case they are used on U.S. troops. They want to be able to detect and perhaps disarm biological weapons before they hurt anyone.

Material scientists play an important role in creating weapons. These scientists use their knowledge of chemistry, physics, and biology to understand why different substances have different properties. They might help with such projects as developing stronger kinds of armor or creating lighter materials for weapons or vehicles.

*The protective materials in tactical vests help keep soldiers safe during combat.*

*Students at the U.S. Military Academy study military topics in addition to regular subjects such as math and science.*

# PREPARING FOR A CAREER

Students interested in pursuing a weapons technology job should begin focusing on math, science, technology, and engineering as early as possible. In college, they can specialize in a particular field of science or engineering. Those who want to work on the most advanced projects usually earn a doctorate.

Some weapons designers begin their science or engineering training as members of the military at one of the service academies, such as the U.S. Military Academy in West Point, New York. Going to one of these academies requires students to commit to serve in the military for a certain number of years. Other weapons designers study at a public or private university.

The U.S. military often pays for members with scientific backgrounds to pursue advanced degrees. Military research labs offer **internships** to students who are still seeking a degree.

A U.S. Navy pilot conducts a test flight of an F-35.

4

# FROM CONCEPT TO REALITY

Test pilot Tony Wilson lowered his F-35 over the sea and approached the aircraft carrier. Wilson's plane was the newest in the U.S. military. On his 2014 test flight, Wilson was attempting the first-ever landing of the F-35 on an aircraft carrier. Navy planes must be able to take off and land safely while carriers are at sea. Wilson completed this mission perfectly, and further tests proved that the F-35 can handle all the demands of flying from a carrier.

The idea for the F-35 first came during the 1990s. It took many years of work to design, build, and test the plane. The F-35 is the most complex military plane ever built. It has stealth technology and is packed with weapons and computers. It can fight other planes, attack ground targets, or carry out reconnaissance. Its sensors can gather information about enemy forces and immediately send it to commanders on the ground or at sea. It can also keep an enemy's radar from detecting it.

## ATTACKING FROM ABOVE

| 1944 | 1947 | 1964 | 1991 | 2006 |
|---|---|---|---|---|
| Germany uses the first jet plane in combat. | A U.S. test plane flies faster than the speed of sound. | The United States flies the SR-71 spy plane, the fastest plane ever built. | U.S. pilots fly the first stealth plane in combat. | The F-35 fighter plane takes its first test flight. |

*The F-117 is also known as the Nighthawk.*

## THE FIRST STEPS

In 2001, the U.S. government gave the job of building the F-35 to
Lockheed Martin, a technology company that makes everything
from airplanes to satellites. Lockheed had previously constructed the
world's first stealth plane, the F-117. Its scientists and engineers had
also built the fastest plane ever, the SR-71 Blackbird. In addition to
Lockheed, two other companies did major work on the F-35, while
another created its engine. All four companies relied on smaller
companies, called subcontractors, to build individual parts for them.

Before a plane can actually be built, however, its creators must
settle on a design. Engineers might sketch out many ideas before
settling on one that will work. They consider aerodynamics, or
how air will flow around the aircraft. They also think about which
features a plane will need in order to meet their goals. The main
goal with the F-35 was to build the fastest stealth plane ever.

# TESTING AND TUNING

The designs for a plane's wings and body are usually tested in two ways. Engineers use a computer simulation that shows how the plane will operate in flight. Project scientists and engineers also build small models of the craft or some of its parts and test them in a wind tunnel. Air blows through the tunnel at different speeds, showing how the plane will react when it flies. The F-35 will fly many kinds of missions, so the engineers needed to take that into account when designing its wings. At times, the plane will fly slowly to bomb ground targets. While fighting other planes, it will fly at top speed.

Engineers who are experts in propulsion helped design the engine for the F-35. Another important concern was deciding what kinds of materials were needed to build the plane and its structure. Materials are especially important with a stealth plane. The F-35's parts fit tightly together to help reduce the reflection of enemy radar. Engineers on the project had to help design new machines that could make some of the parts the plane needed.

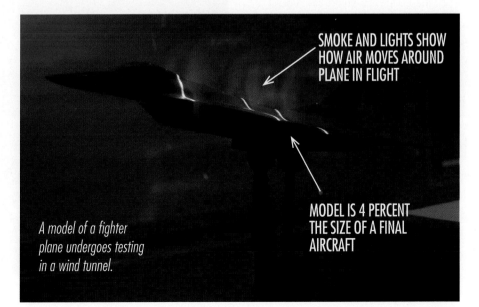

SMOKE AND LIGHTS SHOW HOW AIR MOVES AROUND PLANE IN FLIGHT

MODEL IS 4 PERCENT THE SIZE OF A FINAL AIRCRAFT

*A model of a fighter plane undergoes testing in a wind tunnel.*

# WHERE THE MAGIC HAPPENS

*The AEDC consists of many buildings.*

## BUILDING BETTER AIRCRAFT

When it came time to test the engines for the F-35, the builders went to the Arnold Engineering Development Complex (AEDC) at Arnold Air Force Base in Tennessee. The AEDC has special facilities called propulsion test cells that can check the performance of jet and rocket engines.

## A LONG HISTORY

The AEDC is the largest testing center of its kind in the world. Its scientists and engineers test weapons and spacecraft as well as engines and planes. Some of the center's earliest equipment came from a German testing plant that U.S. forces captured at the end of World War II.

*An F-35 engine undergoes testing at the AEDC.*

Since 1951, the center has been the test site for almost every major U.S. space and weapons program. These projects have included long-range missiles carrying nuclear warheads, satellites, the space shuttle, and all of the country's most advanced military aircraft. Private companies, foreign countries, and universities have also used the AEDC.

An engineer examines an F-35 test model at the AEDC.

## A VARIETY OF TESTS

At the AEDC, civilians with backgrounds in aeronautics, chemistry, mechanical engineering, and other fields worked together with the military to make sure everything operated properly on the F-35. Thousands of hours of testing went on at the center before a plane ever left the ground. Testers at the AEDC can simulate conditions a plane might face at sea level or up to 300 miles (483 km) into space. They can also simulate speeds of up to 20 times the speed of sound.

## DIFFERENT NEEDS FOR DIFFERENT PLANES

There are several versions of the F-35, each with a slightly different engine and each with its own special features. As a result, they had to be tested separately. The Navy F-35, for example, requires more lift power to launch from the short deck of an aircraft carrier. This means the plane needs a more powerful engine than others.

# WORK IN PROGRESS

Lockheed Martin and the other companies that built the F-35 took several years to test the plane's different parts individually before a completed version flew for the first time. As with all engineering projects, there were setbacks and mistakes along the way to creating a finished project. During the testing process, engineers made major changes to the design of one model of the F-35. This version takes off vertically, like a helicopter, rather than gaining speed going down a runway. As a result, it had to be lighter than the others.

The first F-35 prototype was completed in 2006. A prototype is an early version of a completed plane. It contains the desired features but is not the finished product. Test flights of the first F-35 prototype helped engineers make improvements to the plane. Further test flights of the different versions of the plane went on for several years. Lockheed Martin and the other companies building the plane worked closely with the military during these tests. Some tests took place at night. Other tests were conducted to ensure that planes could be refueled in midair.

*A U.S. Marine Corps F-35 lifts off vertically from a ship during a 2015 test flight.*

INFORMATION IS DISPLAYED INSIDE VISOR

*High-tech helmets will make it easier for pilots to operate complex aircraft.*

## LOOKING FORWARD

While flight testing went on, military pilots and civilian computer scientists tested one of the new features of the F-35. Instead of looking at information displayed on the jet's windshield, pilots will see it inside their helmet. If they turn their heads, they'll still be able to see the information. The helmet is designed so it can network with other parts of the plane. It receives images from cameras outside the aircraft so pilots can see in all directions. They can also fire weapons by simply looking at a target. The helmet detects the eyes' direction and then aims the weapon. Pilots each receive custom-made helmets that match up with their vision.

# LASTING CONTRIBUTIONS

*During World War I, bombs were dropped from airplanes by hand.*

## BOMBS OF ALL KINDS

Just before World War I, Germany built the first bomb designed to be dropped from a plane. During that war, several other countries built similar aerial bombs of different sizes. Some weighed up to 2,000 pounds (907 kilograms). The bombs had fins on their end designed to make them fall with their noses pointing down. The nose held a fuse that triggered the explosives when the bomb hit the ground. Since then, bombs have remained important weapons for the world's air forces.

## DOING THINGS DIFFERENTLY

Today's bombs can carry other things besides explosives. Some are filled with chemicals that start a fire when the bomb hits its target. Cluster bombs contain many small explosives that are released as the bomb falls. Each of these smaller explosives is designed to explode over enemy troops just before it reaches the ground.

# BIGGER BLASTS

U.S. warplanes today can carry a wide range of bombs. The simplest ones are not much different from the bombs of World War I. They typically weigh either 500, 1,000, or 2,000 pounds (227, 454, or 907 kg). The largest U.S. bomb weighs 15 tons and is designed to blow up targets that are located underground. Engineers

*Many modern bombs are extremely large and powerful.*

recently built new nuclear bombs that can be set to deliver different size blasts. At the strongest setting, these bombs are three times as powerful as the atomic bombs dropped on Japan in World War II.

# ACCURATE EXPLOSIONS

Other modern bombs can be guided to their targets once they're released. Some follow a laser beam that is aimed at the target. Others have a system inside that relies on the global positioning system (GPS) to navigate. As it falls, this system moves the bomb's tail to steer it toward its target. ✷

*Cluster bombs can cover a large amount of ground with their explosions.*

*Writing and revising computer code takes attention to detail.*

## RISING COSTS

Building a warplane as complex as the F-35 is not easy. Even the best scientists and engineers can't always predict how a plane's systems will work in the real world. Problems with the F-35 delayed its first combat flight for several years. These issues led the U.S. government to spend billions of dollars more than originally planned as engineers worked to find solutions.

One issue was the computer software that controls most of the plane's systems. It was designed to check for problems throughout the plane, but it often failed to notice them. Its creators had written huge amounts of new computer code for the project. Finding and correcting the errors were major tasks.

# TIME FOR TAKEOFF

To address the problems with the software, Lockheed Martin assigned many engineers from other parts of the company to help write new code. The company also made labs available for testing for more than 20 hours a day, giving the team all the time it needed to work on the project.

The U.S. government is counting on the F-35 to be safe for pilots to fly and successfully carry out all its missions. Other countries are also going to fly the F-35. The plane's success is important to them, too.

Thousands of Americans have jobs building the plane's many parts. If problems with the F-35 led the government to cancel the project, these workers would be out of a job, and the government would have wasted a tremendous amount of money on the project. The engineers and scientists behind the F-35 have many people counting on their skills.

A U.S. Marine Corps test pilot climbs into the cockpit of an F-35.

## GLENN L. MARTIN

The "Martin" of Lockheed Martin was Glenn L. Martin (1886–1955), a legendary aeronautics engineer. In 1909, Martin designed and built his own plane. Three years later, he started a company to build aircraft. Martin's company built the first U.S. bomber plane with two engines, giving it more power than others available at the time. After World War II, Martin's company began building missiles and rockets. Since then, it has grown to become one of the world's largest manufacturers of defense technology.

# THE FUTURE

*One day, all military planes might be controlled remotely.*

## TOMORROW'S WEAPONS

The weapons technology of tomorrow will play a huge role in the activities of armed forces around the world. Scientists and engineers will continue developing newer, more powerful weapons. In turn, they will also work to create defenses against these cutting-edge weapons.

## AUTOMATED ARMIES

The pilots of the F-35 may be the last Americans to fly in combat against other planes. In the future, experts expect more warfare to be carried out by remote-controlled vehicles and fully autonomous weapons. These developments will require improvements in the sensors and computers found in today's military equipment.

Aircraft and other traditional vehicles will not be the only remotely operated or autonomous devices on the battlefield. The U.S. government is already testing a four-legged "mule" robot that can carry supplies for soldiers over rocky landscapes. A tiny robotic worm is also in the works. This device is small enough to enter tiny spaces and transmit information about enemy activities back to a base.

*As uncrewed aircraft become more common, fewer pilots will need to risk their lives in combat.*

## SUPERIOR STEALTH

Improvements to underwater military technology will likely be another major focus in the future. Many nations are looking for ways to make submarines harder to detect. This will enable them to get close to enemy targets and launch missiles.

## A NEW KIND OF WARFARE

Being able to defend against cyberattacks will be increasingly important, as well. In the future, cyberwarfare could be used to shut down the computer networks that control everything from electricity and communications to banks and hospitals. U.S. computer scientists in the military and those working for private companies must be able to defend against these attacks.

At the same time, the military will carry out its own attacks against enemy computer networks. ✳

*The Legged Squad Support System is a robot that can carry heavy supplies across a wide variety of terrain.*

# CAREER STATS

## AEROSPACE ENGINEERS

MEDIAN ANNUAL SALARY (2015): $107,830

NUMBER OF JOBS (2014): 72,500

PROJECTED JOB GROWTH, 2014–2024: -2%, a decline

PROJECTED INCREASE IN JOBS, 2014–2024: -1,600

REQUIRED EDUCATION: At least a bachelor's degree

## ELECTRICAL AND ELECTRONIC ENGINEERS

MEDIAN ANNUAL SALARY (2015): $95,230

NUMBER OF JOBS (2014): 315,900

PROJECTED JOB GROWTH, 2014–2024: 0%, little or no change

PROJECTED INCREASE IN JOBS, 2014–2024: -100

REQUIRED EDUCATION: At least a bachelor's degree

## MECHANICAL ENGINEERS

MEDIAN ANNUAL SALARY (2015): $83,590

NUMBER OF JOBS (2014): 277,500

PROJECTED JOB GROWTH, 2014–2024: 5%, as fast as average

PROJECTED INCREASE IN JOBS, 2014–2024: 14,600

REQUIRED EDUCATION: At least a bachelor's degree

*Figures reported by the United States Bureau of Labor Statistics*

# RESOURCES

**BOOKS**

Benoit, Peter. *The Nuclear Age.* New York: Children's Press, 2012.

Bougie, Matt. *Strategic Inventions of the Cold War.* New York: Cavendish Square Publishing, 2016.

Fowler, Will. *The Story of Modern Weapons and Warfare.* New York: Rosen Central, 2012.

Marciniak, Kristin, and Mitchell A. Yockelson. *Fascinating Military Submarines.* Minneapolis: Core Library, 2015.

Mooney, Carla. *Awesome Military Robots.* Minneapolis: Core Library, 2015.

Sheen, Barbara. *Careers in the Military.* San Diego: ReferencePoint Press, 2015.

White, Rowland. *Cleared for Takeoff! The Ultimate Book of Flight.* San Francisco: Chronicle Books, 2013.

**FACTS FOR NOW**

Visit this Scholastic Web site for more information on weapons technology:
**www.factsfornow.scholastic.com**
Enter the keywords **Weapons Technology**

# GLOSSARY

**altitude** (AL-ti-tood) the height of something above the ground or above sea level

**artillery** (ahr-TIL-ur-ee) large, powerful guns

**atoms** (AT-uhmz) the tiniest parts of an element that have all the properties of that element

**autonomous** (aw-TAH-nuh-muhs) able to act independently, without outside control

**bacteria** (bak-TEER-ee-uh) microscopic, single-celled living things that exist everywhere and can either be useful or harmful

**gyroscopes** (JYE-ruh-skohps) devices consisting of a wheel or disk that spins rapidly around an axis that can be tilted in any direction

**internships** (IN-turn-ships) programs where students can learn a skill or job by working with an expert in their field

**nuclear** (NOO-klee-ur) of or having to do with science and technology at the atomic level

**projectiles** (pruh-JEK-tuhlz) objects, such as bullets or missiles, that are thrown or shot through the air

**propulsion** (pruh-PUHL-shuhn) the force by which a vehicle or some other object is pushed along

**reconnaissance** (ruh-KAH-nuh-suhns) the act of observing an area to gain information about it

**shells** (SHELZ) explosive projectiles fired from artillery or other guns

**simulations** (sim-yuh-LAY-shuhnz) trial runs to act out real events; simulations are typically performed using computers

**software** (SAWFT-wair) computer programs that control the workings of the equipment, or hardware, and direct it to do specific tasks

**stealth** (STELTH) the ability to go unseen or undetected

**trajectory** (truh-JEK-tuh-ree) the path a projectile takes while in the air

**turbine** (TUR-buhn) an engine powered by water, steam, wind, or gas passing through the blades of a wheel and making it spin

# INDEX

Page numbers in *italics* indicate illustrations.

# INDEX *(CONTINUED)*

# ABOUT THE AUTHOR

**MICHAEL BURGAN** is the author of more than 250 books for children and young adults, both fiction and nonfiction. His books on science include *Developing Flu Vaccines, Not a Drop to Drink: Water for a Thirsty World,* and biographies of scientists and inventors. A graduate of the University of Connecticut with a degree in history, Burgan is also a produced playwright and the editor of *The Biographer's Craft.* He lives in Santa Fe, New Mexico.